THE UNOFFICIAL BIG GREEN EGG COOKBOOK

THE ULTIMATE COOKBOOK FOR SMOKED MEAT LOVERS, COMPLETE BBQ COOKBOOK FOR SMOKING MEAT, FISH AND VEGETABLES

BY DEAN WOODS

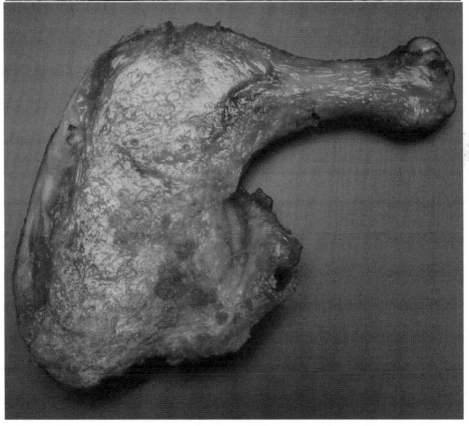

TABLE OF CONTENTS

WHY SMOKING

Smoking is generally used as one of the cooking methods nowadays. The food enriches in protein such as meat would spoil quickly, if cooked for a longer period of time with modern cooking techniques. Whereas, Smoking is a low & slow process of cooking the meat. Where there is a smoke, there is a flavor. With white smoke, you can boost the flavor of your food. In addition to this statement, you can preserve the nutrition present in the food as well. This is flexible & one of the oldest techniques of making food. It's essential for you to brush the marinade over your food while you cook and let the miracle happen. The only thing you need to do is to add a handful of fresh coals or wood chips as and when required. Just taste your regular grilled meat and a smoked meat, you yourself would find the difference. Remember one thing i.e. "Smoking is an art". With a little time & practice, even you can become an expert. Once you become an expert with smoking technique, believe me, you would never look for other cooking techniques. To find one which smoking technique works for you, you must experiment with different woods & cooking methods. Just cook the meat over indirect heat source & cook it for hours. When smoking your meats, it's very important that you let the smoke to escape & move around.

BEEF

MEATBALLS

TOTAL COOK TIME 35 MINUTES

INGREDIENTS FOR 6 SERVINGS

THE MEAT

- Ground beef – 2 pounds

THE RUB

- Garlic powder – 1 tablespoon

- Salt – 1 teaspoon

- Cracked black pepper – 1 teaspoon

- Dried basil – 1 tablespoon

- Dried oregano – 2 teaspoons

- Panko bread crumbs – 1 cup

- Eggs – 2

- Parmesan cheese, grated – 1/4 cup

THE FIRE

- Open all the air vents of the smoker, then fill fire bowl with some charcoal lumps and top with 2-3 wood chunks.

- Light wood chunks with electric smoker starter and wait for 10 to 15 minutes or until smoke starts and charcoals get hot.

- Add some more charcoal lumps and ½ cup wood chips to the firebox, close the lid of the grill, leaving air vents open and wait for 45 minutes or more until temperature reaches to 400 degrees F.

- Once smoker reaches to set temperature, place heat deflector plate on the fire ring with a drip pan on the center and then place the cooking grate on the metal stand.

- Wait for 10 minutes or until smoker heat back to the set temperature level.

METHOD

- In the meantime, prepare meatballs.

- For this, place all the ingredients in a large bowl and stir until well combined.

- Shape mixture into meatballs and place in a baking pan, greased with oil.

- Cover with aluminum foil and place into the heated smoker, in the center of the cooking grill, and cook for 25 minutes.

- Monitor smoking temperature, if the temperature is too high then lower temperature by closing the top air vent or open the top air vent if the temperature is getting lower.

- Then remove foil from pan and continue smoking for 10 minutes or until meatballs are nicely browned.

- When done, remove the pan from the smoker and let meatballs rest in pan for 5 minutes.

- Then transfer meatballs to a plate lined with paper towel to soak excess grease.

- Serve meatballs as desired.

Barbeque Roast Beef

total cook time 1 Hour & 5 Minutes

Ingredients for 6 servings

The Meat

- Beef joint, fat trimmed – 3.3 pounds

The Rub

- Worcestershire sauce – ½ cup
- Salt – 2 teaspoons
- Cracked black pepper – 1 teaspoon

THE FIRE

- Open all the air vents of the smoker, then fill fire bowl with some charcoal lumps and top with 2-3 wood chunks.

- Light wood chunks with electric smoker starter and wait for 10 to 15 minutes or until smoke starts and charcoals get hot.

- Add some more charcoal lumps and ½ cup wood chips to the firebox, close the lid of the grill, leaving air vents open and wait for 45 minutes or more until temperature reaches to 400 degrees F.

- Once smoker reaches to set temperature, place heat deflector plate on the fire ring with a drip pan on the center and then place the cooking grate on the metal stand.

- Wait for 10 minutes or until smoker heat back to the set temperature level.

METHOD

- Before setting the smoker, marinate beef.

- For this, place beef in a large plastic bag and add Worcestershire sauce.

- Seal bag, turn it upside down or until meat is coated with sauce and let marinate for 3 hours in the refrigerator.

- When ready to smoke, remove beef marinate, season with salt and black pepper and place on cooking grate and smoke for 1 hour and 5 minutes or until internal temperature of the meat reaches to 165 degrees F.

- Monitor smoking temperature, if the temperature is too high then lower temperature by closing the top air vent or open the top air vent if the temperature is getting lower.

- When done, remove beef from smoker and let rest for 10 minutes.

- Slice and serve beef with green salad.

BBQ Beef Burger

TOTAL COOK TIME 25 MINUTES

INGREDIENTS FOR 4 SERVINGS

THE MEAT

- Ground Beef – 1 pound

THE RUB

- Salt – ¾ tablespoon
- Cracked black pepper – ¼ teaspoon
- Dried thyme – ½ teaspoon

THE FIRE

- Open all the air vents of the smoker, then fill fire bowl with some charcoal lumps and top with 2-3 wood chunks.

- Light wood chunks with electric smoker starter and wait for 10 to 15 minutes or until smoke starts and charcoals get hot.

- Add some more charcoal lumps and ½ cup wood chips to the firebox, close the lid of the grill, leaving air vents open and wait for 15 minutes or more until temperature reaches to 250 degrees F.

- Once smoker reaches to set temperature, place heat deflector plate on the fire ring with a drip pan on the center and then place the cooking grate on the metal stand.

- Wait for 10 minutes or until smoker heat back to the set temperature level.

METHOD

- In the meantime, place in a large bowl and add remaining ingredients.

- Stir until well combined and then shape mixture into 4 patties.

- Place patties on the cooking grate and smoke for 15 minutes or until cooked through.

- Monitor smoking temperature, if the temperature is too high then lower temperature by closing the top air vent or open the top air vent if the temperature is getting lower.

- Then carefully remove the deflector plate with heat resistant gloves, place the cooking grate back into the smoker, then close the lid and wait until temperature reaches 480 degrees F.

- Place patties on the cooking grate and smoke for 5 minutes per side or until nicely browned and caramelized.

- Serve patties with burger buns.

Smokey Steak

TOTAL COOK TIME 10 MINUTES

INGREDIENTS FOR 10 SERVINGS

THE MEAT

- Steaks – 4

THE RUB

- Salt – ½ tablespoon

- Cracked black pepper – ½ tablespoon

- Cayenne pepper – ½ teaspoon

- Smoked paprika – ½ teaspoon

THE FIRE

- Open all the air vents of the smoker, then fill fire bowl with some charcoal lumps and top with 2-3 wood chunks.

- Light wood chunks with electric smoker starter and wait for 10 to 15 minutes or until smoke starts and charcoals get hot.

- Add some more charcoal lumps and ½ cup wood chips to the firebox, close the lid of the grill, leaving air vents open and wait for 45 minutes or more until temperature reaches to 400 degrees F.

- Once smoker reaches to set temperature, place heat deflector plate on the fire ring with a drip pan on the center and then place the cooking grate on the metal stand.

- Wait for 10 minutes or until smoker heat back to the set temperature level.

Method

- Before setting smoker, let the steak marinade.

- For this stir together salt, cayenne pepper, and paprika and then rub this mixture all over the steaks.

- Let marinate for 45 minutes and then place on the heated cooking grate.

- Close smoker with its lid and grill for 5 minutes.

- Monitor smoking temperature, if the temperature is too high then lower temperature by closing the top air vent or open the top air vent if the temperature is getting lower.

- Then uncover smoker, sprinkle with black pepper, turn steaks and continue smoking for 5 minutes or until done.

- Cook for another 4 to 5 minutes or until steak is cooked to desired doneness.

- Then transfer steaks to serving platters and let rest for 5 minutes before serving.

Smoked Brisket

TOTAL COOK TIME 9 HOURS

INGREDIENTS FOR 7 SERVINGS

THE MEAT

- Beef brisket, fat trimmed – 7 pounds

THE SPICE MIX

- Olive oil – 1/4 cup

- Garlic powder – 2 tablespoons

- Salt – 2 tablespoons

- Cracked black pepper – 2 tablespoons

- White sugar – 2 tablespoons

- Paprika – 2 tablespoons

- Cayenne pepper – 2 tablespoons

- Dried thyme – 1 tablespoon

- Dried rosemary – 1 tablespoon

- Dried oregano – 1 tablespoon

The Spray

- Apple cider vinegar – 1/2 cup

- Apple cider – 1/2 cup

The Fire

- Open all the air vents of the smoker, then fill fire bowl with some charcoal lumps and top with 2-3 wood chunks.

- Light wood chunks with electric smoker starter and wait for 10 to 15 minutes or until smoke starts and charcoals get hot.

- Add some more charcoal lumps and ½ cups wood chips to the firebox, close the lid of the grill, leaving air vents open and wait for 15 minutes or more until temperature reaches to 225 degrees F.

- Once smoker reaches to set temperature, place heat deflector plate on the fire ring with a drip pan on the center and then place the cooking grate on the metal stand.

- Wait for 10 minutes or until smoker heat back to the set temperature level.

METHOD

- Before setting smoker, let beef marinate.

- For this, stir together all the ingredients for spice mix and rub generously all over the beef.

- Wrap this season brisket with plastic wrap, twice, and let marinate for 2 hours in the refrigerator.

- Once smoker reaches to set temperature, place marinated brisket on cooking grate, fat-side down and smoke for 9 hours or until internal temperature of meat reach to 180 degrees F, spraying with the mixture of vinegar and apple juice every 2 hours.

- Monitor smoking temperature, if the temperature is too high then lower temperature by closing the top air vent or open the top air vent if the temperature is getting lower.

- Then carefully wrap brisket with aluminum foil, twice, and continue smoking until internal temperature of brisket reaches to 180 degrees F.

- When done, unwrap brisket and slice to serve.

PORK

BLACKBERRY GLAZED PORK LOIN

TOTAL COOK TIME 1 HOUR AND 12 MINUTES

INGREDIENTS FOR 6 SERVINGS

THE MEAT

- Pork roast, center-cut and fat trimmed – 2 ½ pounds

THE RUB

- Olive oil – ¼ cup

- Pork rub – ¼ cup

THE GLAZE

- Chopped leek – ½ cup

- Butter, unsalted – 1 tablespoon

- Blackberry preserves – ¼ cup

- Apple cider vinegar – 1 ½ tablespoons

- Salt – ¼ teaspoon

- Cracked black pepper – ¼teaspoon

THE FIRE

- Open all the air vents of the smoker, then fill fire bowl with some charcoal lumps and top with 2-3 wood chunks.

- Light wood chunks with electric smoker starter and wait for 10 to 15 minutes or until smoke starts and charcoals get hot.

- Add some more charcoal lumps and ½ cup apple wood chips to the firebox, close the lid of the grill, leaving air vents open and wait for 45 minutes or more until temperature reaches to 425 degrees F.

- Once smoker reaches to set temperature, place a disposable water pan on the firebox filled with 3 cups each of water and apple juice and then place the cooking grate on the metal stand.

- Wait for 15 minutes or until smoker heat back to the set temperature level.

Method

- In the meantime, prepare pork.

- For this, stir together the ingredients of rub and brush generously all over the pork.

- Then place seasoned pork on cooking grate and smoke for 20 minutes.

- Monitor smoking temperature, if the temperature is too high then lower temperature by closing the top air vent or open the top air vent if the temperature is getting lower.

- Then lower temperature to 350 degrees F and continue smoking for 1 hour or until internal temperature of pork reaches to 165 degrees F.

- In the meantime, prepare glaze.

- Place a pan over medium-low heat, add butter and when melted, add leeks.

- Let cook for 3 to 5 minutes or until soft and then whisk in remaining ingredients for glaze until combined.

- Simmer sauce for 5 minutes or more until thickened.

- Then remove the pan from heat and add this brush with sauce all over pork when 15 minutes of smoking time is left.

- When done, remove pork from the smoker, cut into ¼ inch slices and serve.

PORK BELLY

TOTAL COOK TIME 5 HOURS AND 12 MINUTES

INGREDIENTS FOR 4 SERVINGS

THE MEAT

- Pork belly, with skin – 5 pounds

THE SPICE MIX

- White sugar – 1/4 cup

- Salt – 1 tablespoon

- Red chili powder – 1 tablespoon

- Onion powder – 1 tablespoon

- Paprika – 1 teaspoon

- Ground cumin – 1/2 teaspoon

- Cayenne pepper – 1/4 teaspoon

THE HONEY MUSTARD SAUCE

- Minced ginger – 1 tablespoon

- Dried tarragon – 1 tablespoon

- Honey – 1/2 cup

- Ground mustard – 1/4 cup

- Mustard paste – 1/4 cup

- Soy sauce – 1 teaspoon

THE FIRE

- Open all the air vents of the smoker, then fill fire bowl with some charcoal lumps and top with 2-3 wood chunks.

- Light wood chunks with electric smoker starter and wait for 10 to 15 minutes or until smoke starts and charcoals get hot.

- Add some more charcoal lumps and ½ cups wood chips to the firebox, close the lid of the grill, leaving air vents open and wait for 15 minutes or more until temperature reaches to 225 degrees F.

- Once smoker reaches to set temperature, place heat deflector plate on the fire ring with a drip pan on the center and then place the cooking grate on the metal stand.

- Wait for 10 minutes or until smoker heat back to the set temperature level.

METHOD

- In the meantime, prepare pork.

- For this, stir together ingredients for spice mix, rub on the meat of pork belly and let rest until smoker preheats.

- Then plate pork belly on cooking grate and smoke for 4 to 5 hours or until internal temperature of pork reaches to 200 degrees F.

- In the meantime, whisk together all the ingredients for the sauce until well combined and set aside until required.

- Monitor smoking temperature, if the temperature is too high then lower temperature by closing the top air vent or open the top air vent if the temperature is getting lower.

- When done, remove the pork belly from the smoker.

- Carefully remove cooking grate with heat resistant gloves, remove one half of heat deflector plate, then set cast-iron griddle on its place over the direct flame of coals and place a cooking grate over the other half of heat deflector plate.

- Close smoker with its lid and wait until temperature reaches to 400 degrees F.

- In the meantime, use a knife to remove the skin of pork belly and then cut beef into evenly sized rectangle pieces.

- Place these pork pieces on the griddle, fat-side down, and cook for 2 minutes and then transfer them to the cooking grate.

- Baste pork pieces with prepared honey mustard sauce and let smoke for 10 minutes.

- Serve when done.

SMOKED HAM

TOTAL COOK TIME 3 HOURS

INGREDIENTS FOR 6 SERVINGS

THE MEAT

- Pork shoulder, fat trimmed – 3 pounds

THE CURING

- Minced garlic – 3 teaspoons

- Pickling salt – 3 tablespoons

- Brown sugar – ½ cup

- Curing salt – 1 cup

- Water – 2 quarts

THE CURING

- Cracked black pepper – 1 teaspoon

THE FIRE

- Open all the air vents of the smoker, then fill fire bowl with some charcoal lumps and top with 2-3 wood chunks.

- Light wood chunks with electric smoker starter and wait for 10 to 15 minutes or until smoke starts and charcoals get hot.

- Add some more charcoal lumps and ½ cups wood chips to the firebox, close the lid of the grill, leaving air vents open and wait for 15 minutes or more until temperature reaches to 225 degrees F.

- Once smoker reaches to set temperature, place heat deflector plate on the fire ring with a drip pan on the center and then place the cooking grate on the metal stand.

- Wait for 10 minutes or until smoker heat back to the set temperature level.

METHOD

- Before setting smoker, cured pork.

- For this, place all the ingredients for the cure in a large container and stir until salt and sugar are dissolved completely.

- Add pork and let soak for 4 days in the refrigerator.

- Then remove pork from the cure, rinse through and pat dry.

- Season pork with black pepper, then place on cooking grate and smoke for 3 hours or until internal temperature of pork reach to 165 degrees F.

- Monitor smoking temperature, if the temperature is too high then lower temperature by closing the top air vent or open the top air vent if the temperature is getting lower.

- When done, shred pork using two forks, wrap it with aluminum foil and let rest for 30 minutes.

- Serve with a tortilla.

Garlic & Cinnamon Pork Loin Chops

TOTAL COOK TIME 14 Minutes

INGREDIENTS FOR 4 SERVINGS

THE MEAT

- Pork Chops, center-cut – 4

THE RUB

- Garlic powder – 1 tablespoon

- Salt – 4 tablespoon

- Ground black pepper – 2 tablespoons

- Cayenne pepper – 1 tablespoon

- Ground thyme – 2 tablespoons

THE FIRE

- Open all the air vents of the smoker, then fill fire bowl with some charcoal lumps and top with 2-3 wood chunks.

- Light wood chunks with electric smoker starter and wait for 10 to 15 minutes or until smoke starts and charcoals get hot.

- Add some more charcoal lumps and ½ cups wood chips to the firebox, close the lid of the grill, leaving air vents open and wait for 45 minutes or more until temperature reaches to 450 degrees F.

METHOD

- In the meantime, prepare pork chops.

- Stir together ingredients for spice mix and rub all over the chops.

- Once smoker reaches to set temperature, place the cooking grate on the metal stand and then add chops on it.

- Smoke chops for 7 minutes per side or until internal temperature of chops reaches to 165 degrees F.

- Monitor smoking temperature, if the temperature is too high then lower temperature by closing the top air vent or open the top air vent if the temperature is getting lower.

- Serve when ready.

Barbecue Ribs

TOTAL COOK TIME 6 HOURS

INGREDIENTS FOR 6 SERVINGS

THE MEAT

- Baby back ribs, membrane removed – 3 pounds

THE RUB

- Garlic salt – 4 tablespoons
- Salt – 1 tablespoon

- Ground black pepper – 1 tablespoon

- Red chili powder – 2 tablespoons

- Brown sugar – 4 tablespoons

- White sugar – 4 tablespoons

- Cayenne pepper – 1 tablespoon

- Smoked paprika – 1 tablespoon

THE BARBECUE SAUCE

- White onion chopped – 1

- Brown sugar – 2 tablespoons

- Mustard powder – 1 teaspoon

- Tomato purée – 1 tablespoon

- Apple cider vinegar – 2 tablespoons

- Worcestershire sauce – 2 tablespoons

- Olive oil – 2 tablespoons

- Water – 1/2 cup

THE FIRE

- Open all the air vents of the smoker, then fill fire bowl with some charcoal lumps and top with 2-3 wood chunks.

- Light wood chunks with electric smoker starter and wait for 10 to 15 minutes or until smoke starts and charcoals get hot.

- Add some more charcoal lumps and ½ cups wood chips to the firebox, close the lid of the grill, leaving air vents open and wait for 15 minutes or more until temperature reaches to 225 degrees F.

- Once smoker reaches to set temperature, place heat deflector plate on the fire ring with a drip pan on the center and then place the cooking grate on the metal stand.

- Wait for 10 minutes or until smoker heat back to the set temperature level.

METHOD

- Before setting smoker, marinate ribs.

- For this stir together ingredients for spice mix until combined.

- Brush ribs with oil, then season with the spice mix and let marinate in the refrigerator for 6 hours or overnight.

- Then place ribs on smoking grate and smoke for 3 hours.

- Monitor smoking temperature, if the temperature is too high then lower temperature by closing the top air vent or open the top air vent if the temperature is getting lower.

- After 3 hours or smoking, wrap ribs with aluminum foil and continue smoking for 2 hours.

- In the meantime, prepare barbecue sauce.

- Place a saucepan over medium heat, add oil and onion and let cook for 5 minutes or until softened.

- Then stir into tomato puree along with remaining ingredients and simmer sauce for 10 to 15 minutes.

- When done, set sauce aside until required.

- Then unwrap ribs, brush generously with prepared sauce and smoke for another 1 hour.

- Slice and serve ribs with a green salad.

LAMB

Barbecue Lamb Chops

total cook time 18 Minutes

INGREDIENTS FOR 10 SERVINGS

THE MEAT

- Lamb chops – 10

THE MARINADE

- Honey – 2 tablespoons

- Soy sauce – 2 tablespoons

- Worcestershire sauce – 1 tablespoon

- Mustard paste – 1 tablespoon

- Red currant jelly – 2 tablespoons

- Tomato ketchup – 2 tablespoons

THE FIRE

- Open all the air vents of the smoker, then fill fire bowl with some charcoal lumps and top with 2-3 wood chunks.

- Light wood chunks with electric smoker starter and wait for 10 to 15 minutes or until smoke starts and charcoals get hot.

- Add some more charcoal lumps and ½ cups wood chips to the firebox, close the lid of the grill, leaving air vents open and wait for 45 minutes or more until temperature reaches to 400 degrees F.

- Once smoker reaches to set temperature, place heat deflector plate on the fire ring with a drip pan on the center and then place the cooking grate on the metal stand.

- Wait for 10 minutes or until smoker heat back to the set temperature level.

METHOD

- Before setting smoker, let lamb chops marinade.

- For this, whisk together all the ingredients for the marinade.

- Place pork chops in a large plastic bag, add marinade and seal.

- Turn plastic bag upside down until chops are coated with marinade and let marinate for 30 minutes in the refrigerator.

- When smoker reaches to set temperature, place pork chops on cooking grate and smoke for 9 minutes per side or until a meat thermometer reads 165 degrees F.

- Monitor smoking temperature, if the temperature is too high then lower temperature by closing the top air vent or open the top air vent if the temperature is getting lower.

- When done, remove pork chops from smoker and let rest for 5 minutes and then serve.

RACK OF LAMB

TOTAL COOK TIME 2 HOURS AND 30 MINUTES

INGREDIENTS FOR 4 SERVINGS

THE MEAT

- Rack of lamb ribs, membrane removed – 2

The Rub

- Onion powder – 2 tablespoons

- Ginger powder – 2 tablespoons

- Garlic powder – 2 tablespoons

- Sea salt – 2 tablespoons

- Seasoning salt – 2 tablespoons

- Cracked black peppercorns – 2 tablespoons

- Red chili powder – 2 tablespoons

- Smoked paprika – 2 teaspoons

- Cayenne pepper – 1 teaspoon

- Mustard powder – 2 tablespoons

- Chopped basil – 4 tablespoons

- Chopped rosemary – 4 tablespoons

- Oregano – 2 tablespoons

- Chopped thyme – 4 tablespoons

- Ground cumin – 2 tablespoons

Other Ingredients

- Lemons, juiced – 3

- Olive oil – 2 tablespoons

The Fire

- Open all the air vents of the smoker, then fill fire bowl with some charcoal lumps and top with 2-3 wood chunks.

- Light wood chunks with electric smoker starter and wait for 10 to 15 minutes or until smoke starts and charcoals get hot.

- Add some more charcoal lumps and ½ cups wood chips to the firebox, close the lid of the grill, leaving air vents open and wait for 15 minutes or more until temperature reaches to 225 degrees F.

- Once smoker reaches to set temperature, place heat deflector plate on the fire ring with a drip pan on the center and then place the cooking grate on the metal stand.

- Wait for 10 minutes or until smoker heat back to the set temperature level.

METHOD

- Before setting smoker, marinade ribs.

- For this, place all the ingredients for spice mix and stir until combined.

- Coat meat side of ribs with oil and then sprinkle generously with prepared spice mix or until thick layer forms.

- Place rack of ribs on a baking tray, cover with plastic wrap and let marinate for 24 hours in the refrigerator.

- When smoker reaches to set temperature, place ribs onto the cooking grate and smoke for 2 hours or 30 minutes or until cooked through.

- Monitor smoking temperature, if the temperature is too high then lower temperature by closing the top air vent or open the top air vent if the temperature is getting lower.

- Then remove ribs from smoker, wrap in aluminum foil and let rest for 10 minutes.

- Then squeeze lemon juice over ribs, slice and serve.

LEG OF LAMB

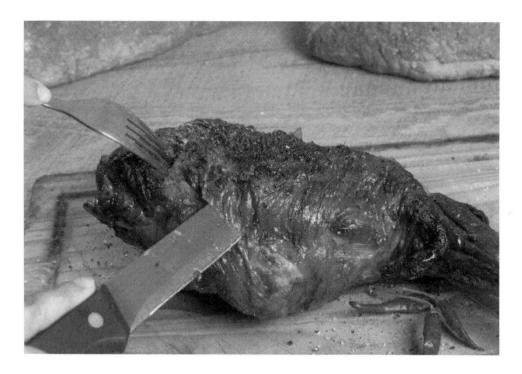

TOTAL COOK TIME 1 HOUR

INGREDIENTS FOR 4 SERVINGS

THE MEAT

- Leg of lamb, fat trimmed – 6.5 pounds

THE RUB

- Minced garlic – 3 teaspoons
- Salt – 2 teaspoons

- Cracked black pepper – 1 teaspoon

- Chopped rosemary – 2 tablespoons

THE FIRE

- Open all the air vents of the smoker, then fill fire bowl with some charcoal lumps and top with 2-3 wood chunks.

- Light wood chunks with electric smoker starter and wait for 10 to 15 minutes or until smoke starts and charcoals get hot.

- Add some more charcoal lumps and ½ cups wood chips to the firebox, close the lid of the grill, leaving air vents open and wait for 30 minutes or more until temperature reaches to 350 degrees F.

- Once smoker reaches to set temperature, place heat deflector plate on the fire ring with a drip pan on the center and then place the cooking grate on the metal stand.

- Wait for 10 minutes or until smoker heat back to the set temperature level.

METHOD

- In the meantime, prepare leg of lamb.

- Season leg of lamb with garlic, salt, black pepper and rosemary and then tie with butcher twine.

- When smoker reaches to set temperature, place leg of lamb on cooking grate and smoke for 1 hour or until internal temperature of lamb reach to 150 degrees F.

- Monitor smoking temperature, if the temperature is too high then lower temperature by closing the top air vent or open the top air vent if the temperature is getting lower.

- Carve leg of lamb and serve.

Lamb Lollipops

total cook time 20 Minutes

Ingredients for 2 servings

The Meat

- Rack of lamb, membrane removed – 1

THE RUB

- Garlic powder – 1 tablespoon

- Ground black pepper – 3 tablespoons

- Cayenne pepper – ½ tablespoon

- Paprika powder – 3 tablespoons

- Dried thyme – 1 tablespoon

- Ground cumin – 1 tablespoon

- Ground nutmeg – ½ tablespoon

BALSAMIC MINT REDUCTION

- Mint Leaves – 3

- Honey – 1/2 cup

- White Balsamic – 1 Cup

- Blackening – 2 teaspoons

THE FIRE

- Open all the air vents of the smoker, then fill fire bowl with some charcoal lumps and top with 2-3 wood chunks.

- Light wood chunks with electric smoker starter and wait for 10 to 15 minutes or until smoke starts and charcoals get hot.

- Add some more charcoal lumps and ½ cups wood chips to the firebox, close the lid of the grill, leaving air vents open and wait for 30 minutes or more until temperature reaches to 325 degrees F.

- Once smoker reaches to set temperature, place cast-iron grate on one side of the fire ring and one half of heat deflector plate on the other side of the fire ring, covered with a cooking grate.

- Wait for 10 minutes or until smoker heat back to the set temperature level.

METHOD

- In the meantime, prepare lamb lollipop.

- For this, place all the ingredients for the rub in a bowl and stir until combined.

- Then rub this mixture generously all over rib slices until well coated.

- When smoke reaches to set temperature, place seasoned slices of ribs on cast-iron grate and smoke for 10 minutes per side until done, don't cover with smoker lid.

- Monitor smoking temperature, if the temperature is too high then lower temperature by closing the top air vent or open the top air vent if the temperature is getting lower.

- In the meantime, prepare mint reduction.

- Place a saucepan over medium heat, add all the ingredients for mint reduction and whisk until blended.

- Bring the sauce to boil, then simmer for 5 minutes and remove the pan from heat.

- Transfer ribs to a plate, drizzle with prepared mint reduction and serve straightaway.

LAMB SHOULDER ROAST

TOTAL COOK TIME 8 HOURS

INGREDIENTS FOR 10 SERVINGS

THE MEAT

- Lamb shoulder, fat trimmed – 5 pounds

THE RUB

- Salt – 1/3 cup

- Ground white pepper – 1 teaspoon

- Brown sugar – 1 1/2 cups

- Cayenne pepper – 2 teaspoons

- Ground cumin – 1 tablespoon

- Dried rosemary – 2 tablespoons

THE FIRE

- Open all the air vents of the smoker, then fill fire bowl with some charcoal lumps and top with 2-3 wood chunks.

- Light wood chunks with electric smoker starter and wait for 10 to 15 minutes or until smoke starts and charcoals get hot.

- Add some more charcoal lumps and ½ cups apple wood chips to the firebox, close the lid of the grill, leaving air vents open and wait for 15 minutes or more until temperature reaches to 225 degrees F.

- Once smoker reaches to set temperature, place heat deflector plate on the fire ring with a drip pan on the center and then place the cooking grate on the metal stand.

- Wait for 10 minutes or until smoker heat back to the set temperature level.

METHOD

- In the meantime, prepare lamb.

- Stir together all the ingredients for the rub, then coat lamb shoulder with this mixture generously and cover with aluminum foil.

- When smoker reaches to set temperature, place covered lamb shoulder onto the smoking grate and smoke for 8 hours or until internal temperature of lamb reach to 165 degrees F.

- Monitor smoking temperature, if the temperature is too high then lower temperature by closing the top air vent or open the top air vent if the temperature is getting lower.

- When done, remove lamb from the smoker, uncover it and slice.

- Serve straightaway.

CHICKEN

WHOLE CHICKEN

TOTAL COOK TIME 1 HOUR AND 30 MINUTES

INGREDIENTS FOR 4 SERVINGS

THE MEAT

- Whole chicken – 3 pounds

OTHER INGREDIENTS

- Salt – 1 teaspoon

- Medium white onion – 1

- Lemon – 1

- Olive oil – 3 tablespoon

THE FIRE

- Open all the air vents of the smoker, then fill fire bowl with some charcoal lumps and top with 2-3 wood chunks.

- Light wood chunks with electric smoker starter and wait for 10 to 15 minutes or until smoke starts and charcoals get hot.

- Add some more charcoal lumps and ½ cups wood chips to the firebox, close the lid of the grill, leaving air vents open and wait for 30 minutes or more until temperature reaches to 350 degrees F.

- Once smoker reaches to set temperature, place heat deflector plate on the fire ring with a drip pan on the center and then place the cooking grate on the metal stand.

- Wait for 10 minutes or until smoker heat back to the set temperature level.

METHOD

- In the meantime, prepare meat.

- For this, massage chicken with olive oil and then sprinkle with salt.

- Peel onion, cut into quarters, cut lemon into quarters and stuff chicken with it.

- Place chicken on the cooking grate and smoke for 1 hour and 30 minutes or until chicken internal temperature reaches to 165 degrees F.

- Monitor smoking temperature, if the temperature is too high then lower temperature by closing the top air vent or open the top air vent if the temperature is getting lower.

- Serve when chicken is cooked through.

Smoked Chicken Breast

total cook time 1 Hour and 38 Minutes

Ingredients for 4 servings

The Meat

- Chicken breast – 4

THE SAUCE

- Sea salt – 1 ½ tablespoons

- Ground black pepper – ½ teaspoon

- Brown sugar – 1 tablespoon

- Sriracha hot sauce – 1 tablespoon

THE FIRE

- Open all the air vents of the smoker, then fill fire bowl with some charcoal lumps and top with 2-3 wood chunks.

- Light wood chunks with electric smoker starter and wait for 10 to 15 minutes or until smoke starts and charcoals get hot.

- Add some more charcoal lumps and ½ cup mesquite wood chips to the firebox, close the lid of the grill, leaving air vents open and wait for 45 minutes or more until temperature reaches to 400 degrees F.

- Once smoker reaches to set temperature, place cast-iron grate on one side of the fire ring and one half of heat deflector plate on the other side of the fire ring, covered with a cooking grate.

- Wait for 10 minutes or until smoker heat back to the set temperature level.

METHOD

- Before setting the smoker, marinate chicken.

- Whisk together all the ingredients for the sauce until well combined and then cover chicken breast with it.

- Then place chicken breasts into a large plastic bag and let marinate for 8 hours in the refrigerator.

- When the smoker has reached to set temperature, place marinated chicken breasts on cast-iron grate and smoke for 4 minutes per side.

- Monitor smoking temperature, if the temperature is too high then lower temperature by closing the top air vent or open the top air vent if the temperature is getting lower.

- Transfer chicken breasts on the cooking grate, over deflector plate and continue smoking for 1 hour and 30 minutes or until internal temperature of chicken reaches to 165 degrees F.

- Slice and serve.

Chicken Legs

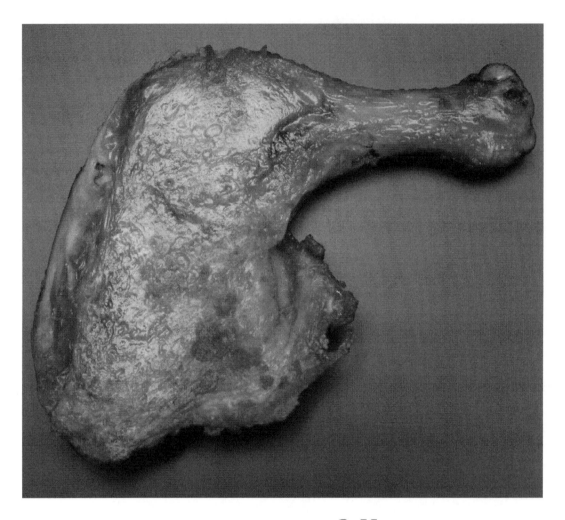

TOTAL COOK TIME 2 HOURS

INGREDIENTS FOR 2 SERVINGS

THE MEAT

- Chicken quarters – 2

The Marinade

- Italian dressing – 2 cups

The Seasoning

- Poultry seasoning – ½ cup

The Barbecue Sauce

- Salt – 1/2 teaspoon

- Cracked black pepper – 1/2 teaspoon

- Brown sugar – 2 tablespoons

- Ground cumin – 1/2 teaspoon

- Ketchup – 1/2 cup

- Apple cider vinegar – 1/4 cup

The Fire

- Open all the air vents of the smoker, then fill fire bowl with some charcoal lumps and top with 2-3 wood chunks.

- Light wood chunks with electric smoker starter and wait for 10 to 15 minutes or until smoke starts and charcoals get hot.

- Add some more charcoal lumps and ½ cups wood chips to the firebox, close the lid of the grill, leaving air vents open and wait for 30 minutes or more until temperature reaches to 300 degrees F.

- Once smoker reaches to set temperature, place heat deflector plate on the fire ring with a drip pan on the center and then place the cooking grate on the metal stand.

- Wait for 10 minutes or until smoker heat back to the set temperature level.

METHOD

- Before setting the smoker, marinate chicken pieces.

- For this, place chicken quarts in a large plastic bag, pour in Italian dressing and seal the bag.

- Turn the bag upside down and let marinate for 4 hours in the refrigerator.

- Then remove chicken pieces from marinade and season with poultry seasoning.

- Place the chicken pieces on cooking grate and smoke for 45 minutes.

- Monitor smoking temperature, if the temperature is too high then lower temperature by closing the top air vent or open the top air vent if the temperature is getting lower.

- In the meantime, prepare barbecue sauce.

- Place pan over medium heat, add all the ingredients for sauce and whisk until well combined.

- Cook sauce for 5 minutes and then set aside until required.

- After 45 minutes of smoking, baste chicken with prepared barbecue sauce until coated thickly.

- Continue smoking for 45 minutes or until internal temperature of chickens reaches to 165 degrees F.

- Then remove chicken pieces from smoker and serve straightaway.

CHICKEN WINGS

TOTAL COOK TIME 1 HOUR AND 5 MINUTES

INGREDIENTS FOR 6 SERVINGS

THE MEAT

- Chicken wings – 3 pounds

Other Ingredients

- Salt – 2 tablespoons

- Cracked black pepper – 2 teaspoons

- Buffalo sauce – ½ cup

- Melted butter – ½ cup

The Fire

- Open all the air vents of the smoker, then fill fire bowl with some charcoal lumps and top with 2-3 wood chunks.

- Light wood chunks with electric smoker starter and wait for 10 to 15 minutes or until smoke starts and charcoals get hot.

- Add some more charcoal lumps and ½ cups wood chips to the firebox, close the lid of the grill, leaving air vents open and wait for 30 minutes or more until temperature reaches to 350 degrees F.

- Once smoker reaches to set temperature, place heat deflector plate on the fire ring with a drip pan on the center and then place the cooking grate on the metal stand.

- Wait for 10 minutes or until smoker heat back to the set temperature level.

Method

- In the meantime, prepare chicken wings.

- Clean chicken wings, pat dry and then season with salt and black pepper.

- Place seasoned chicken wings on cooking grate and smoke for 1 hour.

- Monitor smoking temperature, if the temperature is too high then lower temperature by closing the top air vent or open the top air vent if the temperature is getting lower.

- Switch on the broiler, set temperature to 450 degrees F and let preheat.

- After 1 hour of smoking, transfer chicken wings to a baking sheet in a single layer and broil for 4 to 5 minutes or until crispy.

- Whisk together buffalo sauce and butter until blended, add chicken wings and toss to coat.

- Serve straightaway.

TURKEY

TURKEY BREAST

TOTAL COOK TIME 4 HOURS

INGREDIENTS FOR 6 SERVINGS

THE MEAT

- Turkey breast, boneless – 6 pounds

THE RUB

- Onion salt – 2 teaspoons

- Garlic powder – 1/2 teaspoon

- Salt – 1 ½ teaspoon

- Red chili powder – 2 teaspoons

- Cayenne pepper – 1/4 teaspoon

- Dried oregano – 1 teaspoon

- Ground cumin – 1 teaspoon

- Ground allspice – 1/4 teaspoon

THE BRINE

- Curing salt – 4 teaspoons

- Salt – 1/4 cup

- Sugar – 1/4 cup

- Water – 2 quarts

THE FIRE

- Open all the air vents of the smoker, then fill fire bowl with some charcoal lumps and top with 2-3 wood chunks.

- Light wood chunks with electric smoker starter and wait for 10 to 15 minutes or until smoke starts and charcoals get hot.

- Add some more charcoal lumps and ½ cups wood chips and ½ cup apple wood chips to the firebox, close the lid of the grill, leaving air vents open and wait for 15 minutes or more until temperature reaches to 225 degrees F.

- Once smoker reaches to set temperature, place heat deflector plate on the fire ring with a drip pan on the center and then place the cooking grate on the metal stand.

- Wait for 10 minutes or until smoker heat back to the set temperature level.

METHOD

- Before setting smoker, cure turkey breast.

- For this, stir together all the ingredients for the brine in a large container until salt and sugar dissolve completely.

- Add turkey breast and let soak for 12 hours.

- In the meantime, stir together all the ingredients for rub and set aside until required.

- Then rinse turkey breast, pat dry and rub with the prepared rub.

- When smoker reaches to set temperature, place turkey breast on the cooking grate and smoke for 3 ½ hours to 4 hours or until internal temperature of the turkey reaches to 165 degrees F.

- Monitor smoking temperature, if the temperature is too high then lower temperature by closing the top air vent or open the top air vent if the temperature is getting lower.

- Carve turkey breast and serve.

Citrus Turkey Legs

TOTAL COOK TIME 4 HOURS

INGREDIENTS FOR 3 SERVINGS

THE MEAT

- Turkey legs – 3 pounds

THE MARINADE

- Orange juice – ¼ cup

- Hot sauce – ¼ cup

- Mustard paste – ¼ cup

- Olive oil – ¼ cup

THE SEASONING

- Poultry seasoning – ¼ cup

THE GLAZE

- Orange juice – ¼ cup

- Honey – ¼ cup

- Mustard paste – ¼ cup

- Barbecue sauce – ¼ cup

- Allspice mix – 1/8 teaspoon

THE FIRE

- Open all the air vents of the smoker, then fill fire bowl with some charcoal lumps and top with 2-3 wood chunks.

- Light wood chunks with electric smoker starter and wait for 10 to 15 minutes or until smoke starts and charcoals get hot.

- Add some more charcoal lumps and ½ cups wood chips and apple wood chips to the firebox, close the lid of the grill, leaving air vents open and wait for 15 minutes or more until temperature reaches to 225 degrees F.

- Once smoker reaches to set temperature, place heat deflector plate on the fire ring with a drip pan on the center and then place the cooking grate on the metal stand.

- Wait for 10 minutes or until smoker heat back to the set temperature level.

Method

- Before setting smoker, let turkey legs marinate.

- For this, whisk together all the ingredients of marinade until blended.

- Place turkey legs in a large plastic bag, pour in marinade and seal the bag.

- Turn it upside down until legs are coated with marinade and let marinate in the refrigerator for 8 hours.

- Then remove turkey legs from marinade, season with poultry seasoning, then place on the heated cooking grate and let smoke for 2 to 3 hours.

- Monitor smoking temperature, if the temperature is too high then lower temperature by closing the top air vent or open the top air vent if the temperature is getting lower.

- In the meantime, prepare glaze.

- Place a saucepan over medium heat, all the ingredients for glaze in it and whisk until blended.

- Simmer sauce for 5 minutes and then remove from heat.

- After 45 minutes of smoking time, brush turkey legs with the prepared glaze and smoke until internal temperature reaches to 165 degrees F.

- Brush turkey legs again with prepared glaze and continue smoking for 15 minutes.

- When done, remove turkey legs from smoker and let rest for 10 minutes before serving.

Whole Turkey

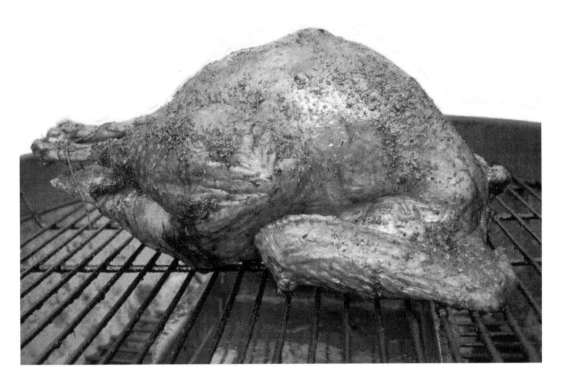

TOTAL COOK TIME 2 HOURS

INGREDIENTS FOR 12 SERVINGS

THE MEAT

- Whole turkey – 12 pounds

THE SAUCE

- Fresh sage, chopped – 2 tablespoons

- Fresh rosemary, chopped – 2 tablespoons

- Fresh thyme, chopped – 2 tablespoons

- Butter, unsalted and softened – 1 cup

- Lemon zest – 2 teaspoons

- Lemon juice – 2 tablespoons

THE FIRE

- Open all the air vents of the smoker, then fill fire bowl with some charcoal lumps and top with 2-3 wood chunks.

- Light wood chunks with electric smoker starter and wait for 10 to 15 minutes or until smoke starts and charcoals get hot.

- Add some more charcoal lumps and ½ cups wood chips to the firebox, close the lid of the grill, leaving air vents open and wait for 30 minutes or more until temperature reaches to 350 degrees F.

- Once smoker reaches to set temperature, place heat deflector plate on the fire ring with a drip pan on the center and then place the cooking grate on the metal stand.

- Wait for 10 minutes or until smoker heat back to the set temperature level.

METHOD

- Before setting smoker, prepare the turkey.

- Place turkey on a cutting board, breast side down, and make a cut at each side of the backbone to remove it.

- Trim off excess skin, run finger to separate meat and skin and then rub inside of meat with prepared butter sauce.

- Brush remaining butter sauce on the outside of the skin, then wrap with plastic wrap, place it in a roasting pan and marinate in the refrigerator for 8 hours.

- Then uncover turkey and place on the heated cooking grate, skin side down, and smoke for 2 hours or until internal temperature of the turkey reaches to 165 degrees F.

- Monitor smoking temperature, if the temperature is too high then lower temperature by closing the top air vent or open the top air vent if the temperature is getting lower.

- When done, wrap turkey with aluminum foil and let rest for 30 minutes.

- Cut off turkey legs, wings and thigh, carve the breast and serve.

FISH

SMOKED SALMON

TOTAL COOK TIME 20 MINUTES

INGREDIENTS FOR 2 SERVINGS

THE MEAT

- Salmon – 1 pound

The Marinade

- Brown sugar – 1/4 cup

- Cracked black pepper – ½ teaspoon

- Soy sauce – 1/4 cup

- Lemons, juiced2

- Olive oil – 1/4 cup

- Water – 1/4 cup

The Fire

- Open all the air vents of the smoker, then fill fire bowl with some charcoal lumps and top with 2-3 wood chunks.

- Light wood chunks with electric smoker starter and wait for 10 to 15 minutes or until smoke starts and charcoals get hot.

- Add some more charcoal lumps and ½ cups wood chips to the firebox, close the lid of the grill, leaving air vents open and wait for 30 minutes or more until temperature reaches to 325 degrees F.

- Once smoker reaches to set temperature, place cooking grate on fire ring and wait for 10 minutes or until smoker heat back to the set temperature level.

Method

- Before setting smoke, let salmon marinade.

- For this, whisk together all the ingredients of marinade until blended.

- Add salmon in a large plastic bag, pour in prepared marinade and seal the bag.

- Turn the plastic bag upside down and let marinate for 2 hours in the refrigerator.

- When smoker reaches to set point, place salmon on cooking grate and cook for 10 minutes per side until done.

- Monitor smoking temperature, if the temperature is too high then lower temperature by closing the top air vent or open the top air vent if the temperature is getting lower.

- Serve when ready.

Mahi Mahi

TOTAL COOK TIME 10 MINUTES

INGREDIENTS FOR 4 SERVINGS

THE MEAT

- Mahi mahi fillets – 1 pound

THE MARINADE

- Italian salad dressing – ½ cup

THE FIRE

- Open all the air vents of the smoker, then fill fire bowl with some charcoal lumps and top with 2-3 wood chunks.

- Light wood chunks with electric smoker starter and wait for 10, to 15 minutes or until smoke starts and charcoals get hot.

- Add some more charcoal lumps and ½ cups wood chips to the firebox, close the lid of the grill, leaving air vents open and wait for 15 minutes or more until temperature reaches to 225 degrees F.

- Once smoker reaches to set temperature, place the cooking grate on the fire ring and wait for 10 minutes or until smoker heat back to the set temperature level.

METHOD

- Before setting smoker, marinate fillets.

- For this, whisk together all the ingredients for marinade in a large bowl, then add fillet and toss until well coated.

- Cover the bowl and let marinate for 1 hour in the refrigerator.

- When smoker reaches to set temperature, place marinated fillets on smoking grate and smoke for 5 minutes per side or until done.

- Monitor smoking temperature, if the temperature is too high then lower temperature by closing the top air vent or open the top air vent if the temperature is getting lower.

- Serve straightaway.

Sweet & Sour Salmon

TOTAL COOK TIME 35 MINUTES

INGREDIENTS FOR 1 SERVINGS

THE MEAT

- Salmon fillet – 1

THE RUB

- Garlic salt – 1 teaspoon

- Ground black pepper – 1/2 teaspoon

- Honey – 1 teaspoon

- Soy sauce – 2 tablespoon

- Olive oil – 2 tablespoons

OTHER INGREDIENTS

- Green beans – 1 pound

- Italian dressing – ½ cup

- Cider plant – 1

THE FIRE

- Open all the air vents of the smoker, then fill fire bowl with some charcoal lumps and top with 2-3 wood chunks.

- Light wood chunks with electric smoker starter and wait for 10 to 15 minutes or until smoke starts and charcoals get hot.

- Add some more charcoal lumps and ½ cups wood chips to the firebox, close the lid of the grill, leaving air vents open and wait for 45 minutes or more until temperature reaches to 400 degrees F.

- Once smoker reaches to set temperature, place heat deflector plate on the fire ring with a drip pan on the center and then place the cooking grate on the metal stand.

- Wait for 10 minutes or until smoker heat back to the set temperature level.

METHOD

- Before setting the smoker, prepare salmon.

- For this, soak cider planks for 30 minutes.

- In the meantime, whisk together garlic salt, black pepper, honey and soy sauce in a bowl until blended, add salmon and toss until well coated.

- Then drizzle oil all over salmon and set aside until required.

- When smoker reaches to set temperature, place soaked cider plant on cooking grate and let grill for 5 minutes or until smoke.

- Turn cider plant, then add salmon, skin-side down, and smoke for 30 minutes, flipping salmon halfway through.

- Toss green beans and Italian dressing in a skillet pan, place it in the smoker and smoke for 30 minutes, stir halfway through.

- Monitor smoking temperature, if the temperature is too high then lower temperature by closing the top air vent or open the top air vent if the temperature is getting lower.

- Serve salmon with green beans.

Tuna Steaks

TOTAL COOK TIME 21 MINUTES

INGREDIENTS FOR 3 SERVINGS

THE MEAT

- Tuna fillets – 3

THE SALSA VERDE

- Basil leaves – 1 cup

- Cloves of garlic, peeled – 2

- Parsley leaves – 1 cup

- Oregano leaves – ¼ cup

- Caper – 2 tablespoons

- Mustard paste – 1 tablespoon

- Olive oil – 1 cup

THE PUREE

- Navy beans – 15 ounce

- Minced garlic – 1 teaspoon

- Cream – ½ cup

- Butter, unsalted – 4 tablespoons

- Salt – 1 teaspoon

- Ground black pepper – ½ teaspoon

THE FIRE

- Open all the air vents of the smoker, then fill fire bowl with some charcoal lumps and top with 2-3 wood chunks.

- Light wood chunks with electric smoker starter and wait for 10 to 15 minutes or until smoke starts and charcoals get hot.

- Add some more charcoal lumps and ½ cups wood chips to the firebox, close the lid of the grill, leaving air vents open and wait for 15 minutes or more until temperature reaches to 225 degrees F.

- Once smoker reaches to set temperature, place the cooking grate on the fire ring and wait for 10 minutes or until smoker heat back to the set temperature level.

METHOD

- Before setting the smoker, marinate tuna.

- For this, place all the ingredients for salsa in a food processor and pulse at high speed until smooth.

- Place half of the salsa in a plastic bag, add tuna and seal the bag, reserve remaining salsa for later use.

- Turn bag upside down until salsa coat tuna and let marinate for 30 minutes in the refrigerator.

- In the meantime, prepare the puree.

- Place a saucepan over medium heat, add beans, garlic, and cream, stir until combined and cook for 15 minutes.

- Then remove the pan from heat, add butter, salt, and black pepper in the pan and puree mixture using stand mixer until smooth, set aside until required.

- When smoker reaches to set temperature, place marinated tuna steaks on cooking grate and smoke for 3 minutes per side or until cooked to desired doneness.

- Monitor smoking temperature, if the temperature is too high then lower temperature by closing the top air vent or open the top air vent if the temperature is getting lower.

- Serve tuna steaks with prepared puree and salsa.

SEAFOOD

GARLIC AND PARSLEY PRAWNS

TOTAL COOK TIME 10 MINUTES

INGREDIENTS FOR 4 SERVINGS

THE MEAT

- Prawns, fresh – 1.3 pounds

THE MARINADE

- Chopped parsley – ¼ cup

- Minced garlic – 1 ½ teaspoon

- Salt - ¼ teaspoon

- Olive oil – 1/3 cup

THE FIRE

- Open all the air vents of the smoker, then fill fire bowl with some charcoal lumps and top with 2-3 wood chunks.

- Light wood chunks with electric smoker starter and wait for 10 to 15 minutes or until smoke starts and charcoals get hot.

- Add some more charcoal lumps and ½ cups wood chips to the firebox, close the lid of the grill, leaving air vents open and wait for 15 minutes or more until temperature reaches to 350 degrees F.

- Once smoker reaches to set temperature, place heat deflector plate on the fire ring with a drip pan on the center and then place the cooking grate on the metal stand.

- Wait for 10 minutes or until smoker heat back to the set temperature level.

Method

- Before setting the smoker, let prawns marinade.

- For this, whisk together all the ingredients for marinade in a large bowl until combined and then add prawns.

- Toss to coat and then let marinate for 1 hour.

- After 1 hour, thread marinade prawns onto sewers, the place onto the heated cooking grate and smoke for 5 minutes per side or until cooked through.

- Monitor smoking temperature, if the temperature is too high then lower temperature by closing the top air vent or open the top air vent if the temperature is getting lower.

- Serve when ready.

PAELLA

TOTAL COOK TIME 3 HOURS & 53 MINUTES

INGREDIENTS FOR 4 SERVINGS

THE MEAT

- Green prawns – 1.1 pound
- Squid rings – ½ pound
- Mussels – 12

THE FISH STOCK

- Small rockfish – 2.2 pounds
- Mussels – 12
- Medium red onion, diced – 1

- Medium tomatoes, quartered – 4

- Olive oil – 2 tablespoons

- Water – 4 ½ cups

THE TOMATO SAUCE

- Medium red onion, diced – 1 1/2

- Minced garlic – 2 teaspoons

- Crushed tomatoes – 3.3 pounds

- Olive oil – 4 tablespoons

OTHER INGREDIENTS

- Arborio rice, rinsed – 1 ¼ cups

THE FIRE

- Open all the air vents of the smoker, then fill fire bowl with some charcoal lumps and top with 2-3 wood chunks.

- Light wood chunks with electric smoker starter and wait for 10 to 15 minutes or until smoke starts and charcoals get hot.

- Add some more charcoal lumps with ½ cup of wood chips to the firebox, close the lid of the grill, leaving air vents open and wait for 15 minutes or more until temperature reaches to 225 degrees F.

- Once smoker reaches to set temperature, place heat deflector plate on the fire ring with a drip pan on the center and then place the paella pan on the metal stand.

- Wait for 10 minutes or until smoker heat back to the set temperature level.

METHOD

- Before setting smoker, prepare fish stock and tomato sauce.

- For fish stock, place a large saucepan over medium heat, add oil and when heated, add onion.

- Cook for 10 to 15 minutes or until softened, then add remaining ingredients for fish stock and stir until mixed.

- Bring the mixture to boil and cook for 3 hours, pan uncovered.

- Then pass the stock through a sieve and collect liquid in a bowl, set aside until required.

- While stock cooks, prepare tomato sauce.

- Place another medium saucepan over medium heat, add oil and when heated, add onions.

- Cook for 15 minutes or until tender and nicely golden brown.

- Then reserve ½ of cooked onion and add garlic into the pan.

- Continue cooking for 5 minutes, then stir in tomatoes and cook for 1 hour, over low heat.

- Remove saucepan from heat when tomato sauce is cooked.

- On heated paella pan, place reserved onion along with half of the tomato sauce and cook for 5 minutes.

- Add prawns, squid, mussels, and rice and cook for 3 minutes.

- Pour in fish stock, stir until well combined and smoke for 25 minutes.

- Monitor smoking temperature, if the temperature is too high then lower temperature by closing the top air vent or open the top air vent if the temperature is getting lower.

- Serve straight away.

SCALLOP FILLED CHICKEN BREAST

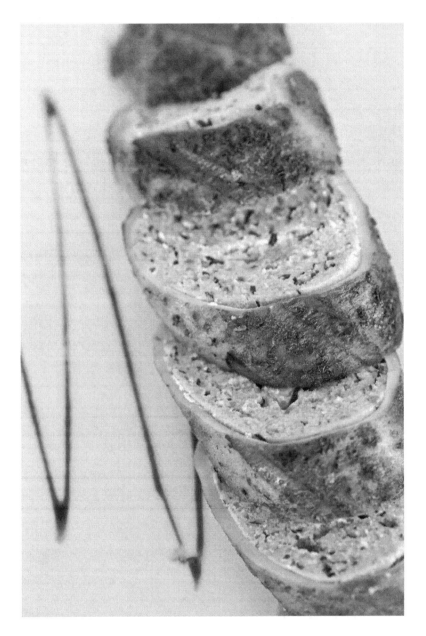

TOTAL COOK TIME 13 MINUTES

INGREDIENTS FOR 2 SERVINGS

THE MEAT

- Chicken breast, halved – 1
- Scallops, well cleaned – 10
- Slices of smoked ham – 2

THE RUB

- Garlic powder – 1 teaspoon
- Sea salt – 1/2 teaspoon
- Ground black pepper – 1/4 teaspoon
- Smoked paprika – 1/2 teaspoon
- Ground cumin – 1 teaspoon
- Ground coriander – 1/2 teaspoon
- Olive oil – 2 tablespoons

OTHER INGREDIENTS

- Spinach leaves – ¼ cup
- Salt – ½ teaspoon
- Cracked black pepper – ½ teaspoon
- Olive oil – 2 tablespoons

The Fire

- Open all the air vents of the smoker, then fill fire bowl with some charcoal lumps and top with 2-3 wood chunks.

- Light wood chunks with electric smoker starter and wait for 10 to 15 minutes or until smoke starts and charcoals get hot.

- Add some more charcoal lumps and ½ cups wood chips to the firebox, close the lid of the grill, leaving air vents open and wait for 45 minutes or more until temperature reaches to 400 degrees F.

- Once smoker reaches to set temperature, place heat deflector plate on the fire ring with a drip pan on the center and then place the paella pan on the metal stand.

- Wait for 10 minutes or until smoker heat back to the set temperature level.

Method

- In the meantime, prepare chicken.

- For this, chop cleaned scallop, then place in a bowl, add olive oil and toss until coated.

- Make pocket into the chicken by slicing into the half but do not cut all the way through and then season pocket with salt and black pepper.

- Stir together ingredients for rub and then sprinkle generously on the outside of chicken.

- Stuff a slice of ham, half of spinach and scallops into the chicken pocket and then use aluminum foil to roll it and tighten the ends.

- Stuff remaining chicken breast half in the same manner and wrap with aluminum foil.

- Place the covered chicken breast on cooking grate and smoke for 10 minutes, turning chicken every 2 minutes.

- Monitor smoking temperature, if the temperature is too high then lower temperature by closing the top air vent or open the top air vent if the temperature is getting lower.

- Unwrap chicken breast and continue smoking for 3 minutes.

- Slice and serve.

Parmesan Shrimp

TOTAL COOK TIME 10 MINUTES

INGREDIENTS FOR 6 SERVINGS

THE MEAT

- Large shrimps, peeled and deveined – 1 ½ pounds

The Cocktail Sauce

- Chopped cilantro – 1 tablespoon

- Prepared horseradish – 2 tablespoons

- Salt – 1 teaspoon

- Cracked black pepper – ½ teaspoon

- Ketchup – 1 cup

- Worcestershire sauce – 2 teaspoon

- Lime juice – 1 teaspoon

Other Ingredients

- Chopped cilantro – 2 tablespoons

- Minced garlic – 1 teaspoon

- Salt – 1 teaspoon

- Cracked black pepper – ½ teaspoon

- Lime, juiced – 2

- Olive oil – 2 tablespoons

- Grated parmesan cheese – ½ cup

- Spaghetti, boiled – for serving

The Fire

- Open all the air vents of the smoker, then fill fire bowl with some charcoal lumps and top with 2-3 wood chunks.

- Light wood chunks with electric smoker starter and wait for 10 to 15 minutes or until smoke starts and charcoals get hot.

- Add some more charcoal lumps and ½ cups wood chips to the firebox, close the lid of the grill, leaving air vents open and wait for 45 minutes or more until temperature reaches to 400 degrees F.

- Once smoker reaches to set temperature, place heat deflector plate on the fire ring with a drip pan on the center and then place the cooking grate on the metal stand.

- Wait for 10 minutes or until smoker heat back to the set temperature level.

METHOD

- In the meantime, place garlic, salt, black pepper, cheese, lime juice and oil in a large bowl and whisk until combined.

- Add shrimps, toss to coat and then place shrimps on a baking sheet in a single layer.

- Place this baking sheet on cooking grate and smoke for 10 minutes or until shrimps are pink.

- In the meantime, prepare the cocktail sauce.

- For this, stir together all the ingredients for the sauce until well combined, then cover the bowl with lid and let rest in the refrigerator until required.

- Monitor smoking temperature, if the temperature is too high then lower temperature by closing the top air vent or open the top air vent if the temperature is getting lower.

- Serve shrimps with prepared cocktail sauce and boiled spaghetti.

GAME & RABBIT

CORNISH HENS

TOTAL COOK TIME 2 HOURS

INGREDIENTS FOR 2 SERVINGS

THE MEAT

- Cornish hens – 2

THE BRINE

- Water, chilled – 8 cups

- Salt – ½ cup

- Brown sugar – ½ cup

THE RUB

- Salt – 2 tablespoons

- Ground black pepper – 2 tablespoons

- White sugar – 2 tablespoons

- Brown sugar – 2 tablespoons

- Ground cumin – 2 tablespoons

- Red chili powder – 2 tablespoons

- Cayenne pepper – 1 tablespoon

- Paprika – 1/4 cup

THE FIRE

- Open all the air vents of the smoker, then fill fire bowl with some charcoal lumps and top with 2-3 wood chunks.

- Light wood chunks with electric smoker starter and wait for 10 to 15 minutes or until smoke starts and charcoals get hot.

- Add some more charcoal lumps and ½ cups apple wood chips to the firebox, close the lid of the grill, leaving air vents open and wait for 45 minutes or more until temperature reaches to 350 degrees F.

- Once smoker reaches to set temperature, place heat deflector plate on the fire ring with a drip pan on the center and then place the cooking grate on the metal stand.

- Wait for 10 minutes or until smoker heat back to the set temperature level.

METHOD

- Before setting the smoker, prepare Cornish hens.

- For this, place all the ingredients for the brine in a large container and stir until salt and sugar are dissolved completely.

- Add hens to the brine, cover the container and let soak for 8 hours in the refrigerator.

- Then remove hens from brine, rinse thoroughly and pat dry.

- Stir together all the ingredients for rub and sprinkle generously all over hens.

- When smoker reached to set temperature, place seasoned hens on cooking grate and smoke for 2 hours or until internal temperature of hens reaches to 165 degrees F.

- Monitor smoking temperature, if the temperature is too high then lower temperature by closing the top air vent or open the top air vent if the temperature is getting lower.

- Serve straightaway.

Smoked Rabbit

TOTAL COOK TIME 2 HOURS

INGREDIENTS FOR 10 SERVINGS

THE MEAT

- Rabbit, gutted – 10 pounds

THE RUB

- Onion Powder – 1/2 tablespoon

- Garlic Powder – 1 tablespoon

- Salt – 1 tablespoon

- Ground Black Pepper – 1 tablespoon

- Cayenne Pepper – 1 tablespoon
- Paprika – ½ tablespoon

THE BRINE

- Fresh parsley – 1 cup
- Salt – 2 tablespoons
- Ground black pepper – 1 teaspoon
- White vinegar – 1/4 cup
- Apple cider vinegar – ¼ cup
- Red wine vinegar – ¼ cup
- Water – 2 cup

OTHER INGREDIENTS

- Slices of bacon - 16 ounce
- Medium white onion, cut in quarters – 1
- Salt – 2 tablespoons
- Olive oil – ¼ cup
- Barbecue sauce – ½ cup

THE FIRE

- Open all the air vents of the smoker, then fill fire bowl with some charcoal lumps and top with 2-3 wood chunks.
- Light wood chunks with electric smoker starter and wait for 10 to 15 minutes or until smoke starts and charcoals get hot.

- Add some more charcoal lumps and ½ cups cherry wood chips to the firebox, close the lid of the grill, leaving air vents open and wait for 15 minutes or more until temperature reaches to 250 degrees F.

- Once smoker reaches to set temperature, place the cooking grate on the fire ring and wait for 10 minutes or until smoker heat back to the set temperature level.

METHOD

- Before setting smoker, prepare rabbit.

- For this, stir together all the ingredients of brine in a large container until salt dissolves.

- Add rabbit and let soak for 1 hour.

- Then remove rabbit from brine, rinse thoroughly and pat dry.

- Stir together all the ingredients for rub until combined.

- Coat rabbit with oil and then sprinkle prepared spice mix all over the rabbit.

- Stuff rabbit with onion, wrap with bacon, secure with butcher twine and sprinkle more with the prepared rub.

- When smoker reached to set temperature, place wrapped rabbit on cooking grate and smoke for 2 hours or until internal temperature of rabbit reaches to 165 degrees F.

- Monitor smoking temperature, if the temperature is too high then lower temperature by closing the top air vent or open the top air vent if the temperature is getting lower.

- Brush rabbit with barbecue sauce every 5 minutes in the last 20 minutes of smoking.

- Slice rabbit and serve.

SMOKED DUCK BREAST

TOTAL COOK TIME 20 MINUTES

INGREDIENTS FOR 4 SERVINGS

THE MEAT

- Duck breast, with skin – 2

THE SEASONING

- Salt – 2 tablespoons

- Cracked black pepper – 1 teaspoon

THE CHERRY SAUCE

- Sweet dark cherries – 12 ounce
- Brown sugar – 2 tablespoons
- Red pepper flakes – ½ teaspoon
- Port – ¼ cup
- Cornstarch – 1 tablespoon
- Lemon juice – 1 tablespoon

THE FIRE

- Open all the air vents of the smoker, then fill fire bowl with some charcoal lumps and top with 2-3 wood chunks.
- Light wood chunks with electric smoker starter and wait for 10 to 15 minutes or until smoke starts and charcoals get hot.
- Add some more charcoal lumps and ½ cups wood chips to the firebox, close the lid of the grill, leaving air vents open and wait for 45 minutes or more until temperature reaches to 350 degrees F.
- Once smoker reaches to set temperature, place the cooking grate on the fire ring and wait for 10 minutes or until smoker heat back to the set temperature level.

METHOD

- In the meantime, prepare duck.
- Use a sharp knife to make the criss-cross pattern all over the skin of ducks and then season with salt and black pepper.
- When smoker reaches to set temperature, place duck on cooking grate, skin side down, and smoke for 20 minutes or until internal

temperature of duck reach to 135 degrees F, turning duck breast every 4 minutes.

- Monitor smoking temperature, if the temperature is too high then lower temperature by closing the top air vent or open the top air vent if the temperature is getting lower.

- While duck smokes, place all the ingredients for sauce in a saucepan, stir until mixed and bring to boil over medium heat.

- Then reduce heat to low and simmer sauce until thickened.

- Cut duck breast into slices and serve with cherry sauce.

ORANGE GLAZED DUCK

TOTAL COOK TIME 2 HOURS AND 30
MINUTES

Ingredients for 4 servings

The Meat

- Whole Duck – 1

The Orange Glaze

- Chopped Serrano pepper – 1

- Salt – 1 teaspoon

- Ground black pepper – ½ teaspoon

- Raw turbinado sugar – 1 cup

- Honey – 1/4 cup

- Coriander seeds – 1 tablespoon

- Orange zest – 1 tablespoon

- Apple cider vinegar – 2 tablespoons

- Butter, unsalted – 1 tablespoon

- Orange liqueur – 1/4 cup

- Orange juice – 1/2 cup

- Chicken stock – 1/2 cup

The Fire

- Open all the air vents of the smoker, then fill fire bowl with some charcoal lumps and top with 2-3 wood chunks.

- Light wood chunks with electric smoker starter and wait for 10 to 15 minutes or until smoke starts and charcoals get hot.

- Add some more charcoal lumps and ½ cups wood chips to the firebox, close the lid of the grill, leaving air vents open and wait for 45 minutes or more until temperature reaches to 375 degrees F.

- Once smoker reaches to set temperature, place heat deflector plate on the fire ring with a drip pan on the center and then place the cooking grate on the metal stand.

- Wait for 10 minutes or until smoker heat back to the set temperature level.

METHOD

- While smoker preheats, prepare orange glaze.

- Place a saucepan over medium heat, add all the ingredients for glaze except for sugar, salt, honey and orange zest.

- Bring the mixture to boil and then stir in salt and sugar until dissolved completely.

- Then stir in honey, add peppers and simmer sauce for 10 to 15 minutes or until thickened.

- When done, remove the pan from heat and let the sauce cool completely.

- When the smoker reached to set temperature, place duck on the cooking grate and let smoke for 2 hours and 30 minutes or until internal temperature of smoke reach to 165 degrees F.

- Monitor smoking temperature, if the temperature is too high then lower temperature by closing the top air vent or open the top air vent if the temperature is getting lower.

- Brush duck with prepared glaze every 30 minutes.

- Serve when ready.

Smoked Venison Roast

TOTAL COOK TIME 1 HOUR AND 30 MINUTES

INGREDIENTS FOR 4 SERVINGS

THE MEAT

- Venison roast – 4 pounds

THE RUB

- Cajun seasoning – 3 tablespoons

- Ground black pepper – 1 tablespoon

- Salt – 1/2 tablespoon

- Minced garlic – 1 tablespoon

- Onion flakes – 1/2 tablespoon

- Olive oil – 6 tablespoons

The Fire

- Open all the air vents of the smoker, then fill fire bowl with some charcoal lumps and top with 2-3 wood chunks.

- Light wood chunks with electric smoker starter and wait for 10 to 15 minutes or until smoke starts and charcoals get hot.

- Add some more charcoal lumps and ½ cups wood chips to the firebox, close the lid of the grill, leaving air vents open and wait for 30 minutes or more until temperature reaches to 300 degrees F.

- Once smoker reaches to set temperature, place the cooking grate on the fire ring and wait for 10 minutes or until smoker heat back to the set temperature level.

Method

- In the meantime, prepare venison.

- For this, place all the ingredients for the rub in a bowl and stir until smooth paste comes together and coat venison with this paste generously.

- When smoker reached to set temperature, place wrapped venison on cooking grate and smoke for 1 hour and 30 minutes or until internal temperature of venison reaches to 165 degrees F.

- Monitor smoking temperature, if the temperature is too high then lower temperature by closing the top air vent or open the top air vent if the temperature is getting lower.

- When done, remove venison from smoker and let rest for 10 minutes.

- Carve venison and serve.

VEGETABLES & SNACKS

MISO MARINATED MUSHROOMS

TOTAL COOK TIME 20 MINUTES

INGREDIENTS FOR 4 SERVINGS

THE VEGETABLE

- Button mushrooms – 20

THE MARINADE

- Brown sugar – 2 tablespoons
- Brown miso paste – 2 tablespoons

- Soy sauce – 1 tablespoon

- Lemon juice – 2 tablespoons

THE FIRE

- Open all the air vents of the smoker, then fill fire bowl with some charcoal lumps and top with 2-3 wood chunks.

- Light wood chunks with electric smoker starter and wait for 10 to 15 minutes or until smoke starts and charcoals get hot.

- Add some more charcoal lumps and ½ cups wood chips to the firebox, close the lid of the grill, leaving air vents open and wait for 45 minutes or more until temperature reaches to 350 degrees F.

- Once smoker reaches to set temperature, place heat deflector plate on the fire ring with a drip pan on the center and then place the cooking grate on the metal stand.

- Wait for 10 minutes or until smoker heat back to the set temperature level.

METHOD

- In the meantime, prepare mushrooms.

- Place all the ingredients for marinade in a bowl and whisk until smooth.

- When the smoker reaches to set temperature, dunk a mushroom into the marinade, then place on cooking grate and smoke mushrooms for 20 minutes.

- Monitor smoking temperature, if the temperature is too high then lower temperature by closing the top air vent or open the top air vent if the temperature is getting lower.

- Serve straight away.

Sweet Potato Mash

TOTAL COOK TIME 1 HOUR

INGREDIENTS FOR 4 SERVINGS

THE VEGETABLE

- Large sweet potato – 2
- Large potatoes, peeled – 6

OTHER INGREDIENTS

- Salt – ½ teaspoon

- Cracked black pepper – ½ teaspoon

- Butter, unsalted – 1 tablespoon

- Milk – ½ cup

THE FIRE

- Open all the air vents of the smoker, then fill fire bowl with some charcoal lumps and top with 2-3 wood chunks.

- Light wood chunks with electric smoker starter and wait for 10 to 15 minutes or until smoke starts and charcoals get hot.

- Add some more charcoal lumps and ½ cups wood chips to the firebox, close the lid of the grill, leaving air vents open and wait for 45 minutes or more until temperature reaches to 350 degrees F.

- Once smoker reaches to set temperature, place heat deflector plate on the fire ring with a drip pan on the center and then place the cooking grate on the metal stand.

- Wait for 10 minutes or until smoker heat back to the set temperature level.

METHOD

- In the meantime, prepare sweet potatoes.

- Wash potatoes until cleaned, pat dry, then pierce them with a fork and wrap with aluminum foil, twice.

- When smoker reached to set temperature, place wrapped sweet potatoes on cooking grate and smoke for 1 hour or until tender.

- Monitor smoking temperature, if the temperature is too high then lower temperature by closing the top air vent or open the top air vent if the temperature is getting lower.

- When done, remove sweet potatoes from smoker and unwrap them.

- Remove their skins, chop into pieces and place in a bowl.

- Add remaining ingredients to sweet potatoes and mash with a fork until smooth.

- Serve immediately.

GRILLED VEGETABLES

TOTAL COOK TIME 8 MINUTES

INGREDIENTS FOR 4 SERVINGS

THE VEGETABLES

- Eggplants – 2
- Zucchini – 3
- Red bell pepper – 1
- Yellow bell pepper – 1

The Pesto

- Toasted hazelnuts – ¼ cup

- Basil leaves – ¼ cup

- Clove of garlic, peeled – 1

- Sea salt – ½ teaspoon

- Olive oil – ¼ cup

- Lemon juice – 1 teaspoon

Other Ingredient

- Salt – 1 tablespoon

The Fire

- Open all the air vents of the smoker, then fill fire bowl with some charcoal lumps and top with 2-3 wood chunks.

- Light wood chunks with electric smoker starter and wait for 10 to 15 minutes or until smoke starts and charcoals get hot.

- Add some more charcoal lumps and ½ cups wood chips to the firebox, close the lid of the grill, leaving air vents open and wait for 45 minutes or more until temperature reaches to 300 degrees F.

- Once smoker reaches to set temperature, place the cooking grate on the fire ring and wait for 10 minutes or until smoker heat back to the set temperature level.

Method

- Before setting the smoker, prepare vegetables.

- Remove top of eggplants and zucchini and slice thinly, lengthwise, about ¼-inch thick.

- Then place these sliced vegetables in a colander, sprinkle with salt, toss and let rest for 30 minutes.

- Then rinse slices of eggplant and zucchini thoroughly and pat dry.

- When smoker reached to set temperature, place slices of eggplant and zucchini on cooking grate and let smoke for 4 minutes per side or until seared and caramelized and peppers are slightly charred.

- Monitor smoking temperature, if the temperature is too high then lower temperature by closing the top air vent or open the top air vent if the temperature is getting lower.

- When done, transfer the vegetables to a serving plate, drizzle with salsa and serve with flatbread.

Whole Corns

TOTAL COOK TIME 30 MINUTES

INGREDIENTS FOR 3 SERVINGS

THE VEGETABLE

- Whole corn, soaked in water – 3

OTHER INGREDIENTS

- Salt – 1 teaspoon

- Cracked black pepper – 1 teaspoon

- Butter, melted – 1 /4 cup

THE FIRE

- Open all the air vents of the smoker, then fill fire bowl with some charcoal lumps and top with 2-3 wood chunks.

- Light wood chunks with electric smoker starter and wait for 10 to 15 minutes or until smoke starts and charcoals get hot.

- Add some more charcoal lumps and ½ cups wood chips to the firebox, close the lid of the grill, leaving air vents open and wait for 45 minutes or more until temperature reaches to 400 degrees F.

- Once smoker reaches to set temperature, place heat deflector plate on the fire ring with a drip pan on the center and then place the cooking grate on the metal stand.

- Wait for 10 minutes or until smoker heat back to the set temperature level.

METHOD

- When smoker reached to set temperature, remove corn from water, place on cooking grate and smoke for 15 minutes.

- Monitor smoking temperature, if the temperature is too high then lower temperature by closing the top air vent or open the top air vent if the temperature is getting lower.

- Then remove corn from the smoker, peel the husk, don't remove it and wash to remove stringy bits from all silks.

- Then season corn with salt, black pepper, brush with butter and pull the husk over corn.

- Tie corn with butcher twine, then return it on cooking grate and smoke for 15 minutes, turning corn every 5 minutes.

- Serve when ready.

Stuffed Peppers

Total Cook Time 1 Hour and 40 Minutes

Ingredients for 6 servings

The Vegetable

- Large bell pepper – 6

The Meat

- Ground beef – 1 pound

Other Ingredients

- Diced tomatoes – 1 ¼ cup

- White onion, chopped – 1

- Minced garlic – 1 teaspoon

- Salt 1 ½ teaspoon

- Cracked black pepper – ¾ teaspoon

- Zatarain's dirty rice mix – 1 cup

- Butter, unsalted – 2 tablespoons

- Shredded cheddar cheese – 2 cups

- Water – 2 1/2 cups

The Fire

- Open all the air vents of the smoker, then fill fire bowl with some charcoal lumps and top with 2-3 wood chunks.

- Light wood chunks with electric smoker starter and wait for 10 to 15 minutes or until smoke starts and charcoals get hot.

- Add some more charcoal lumps and ½ cups wood chips to the firebox, close the lid of the grill, leaving air vents open and wait for 15 minutes or more until temperature reaches to 225 degrees F.

- Once smoker reaches to set temperature, place heat deflector plate on the fire ring with a drip pan on the center and then place the cooking grate on the metal stand.

- Wait for 10 minutes or until smoker heat back to the set temperature level.

Method

- Before setting smoker, prepare stuff pepper.

- For this, place a large skillet pan over medium heat, add 1 tablespoon butter and when melted, add onions.

- Let cook for 5 minutes or until softened and then remove from pan.

- Add remaining butter to the pan and when melted, add beef and cook for 7 to 10 minutes or until beef is nicely browned.

- Drain the fat from beef, add remaining ingredients and stir until well mixed.

- Simmer mixture for 25 minutes or until rice is tender, then remove the pan from heat, and fluff rice with a fork.

- Remove stem and core from each bell pepper, rinse thoroughly, pat dry and then fill with rice mixture.

- Place stuffed peppers in the refrigerator until smoker reaches to set temperature.

- Then place peppers on cooking grate and smoke for 45 to 60 minutes or until cooked through and skin of peppers wrinkles.

- Monitor smoking temperature, if the temperature is too high then lower temperature by closing the top air vent or open the top air vent if the temperature is getting lower.

- Serve immediately.

BAKED APPLES

TOTAL COOK TIME 31 MINUTES

INGREDIENTS FOR 4 SERVINGS

THE FRUIT

- Apples – 3

OTHER INGREDIENTS

- Ground Cinnamon – 2 teaspoons

- Brown Sugar – 3 tablespoons

- Butter, unsalted – 1 tablespoon

- Apple Juice – ½ cup

THE FIRE

- Open all the air vents of the smoker, then fill fire bowl with some charcoal lumps and top with 2-3 wood chunks.

- Light wood chunks with electric smoker starter and wait for 10 to 15 minutes or until smoke starts and charcoals get hot.

- Add some more charcoal lumps and ½ cups wood chips to the firebox, close the lid of the grill, leaving air vents open and wait for 45 minutes or more until temperature reaches to 450 degrees F.

- Once smoker reaches to set temperature, place heat deflector plate on the fire ring with a drip pan on the center and then place the cooking grate on the metal stand.

- Wait for 10 minutes or until smoker heat back to the set temperature level.

METHOD

- In the meantime, prepare apples.

- Cut apples into wedges, arrange them in a baking dish and sprinkle with cinnamon.

- Place butter in a heatproof bowl and microwave for 1 minute or more until melt completely.

- Whisk in sugar until smooth and then drizzle with mixture all over the apples.

- Stir to coat and then evenly pour in apple juice.

- Place the baking sheet on cooking grate and smoke for 30 minutes or until cooked to desired firmness, stirring halfway through.

- Monitor smoking temperature, if the temperature is too high then lower temperature by closing the top air vent or open the top air vent if the temperature is getting lower.

- Serve immediately.

CONCLUSION

I can't express how honored I am to think that you found my book interesting and informative enough to read it all through to the end. I thank you again for purchasing this book and I hope that you had as much fun reading it as I had writing it. I bid you farewell and encourage you to move forward and find your true Smoked Meat spirit!

GET YOUR FREE GIFT

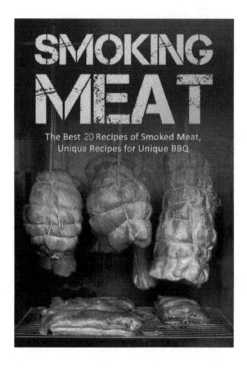

Suscribe to our Mail List and get your FREE copy of the book

'Smoking Meat: The Best 20 Recipes of Smoked Meat, Unique Recipes for Unique BBQ'

https://tiny.cc/smoke20

MY OTHER BOOKS

FOR PORK LOVERS

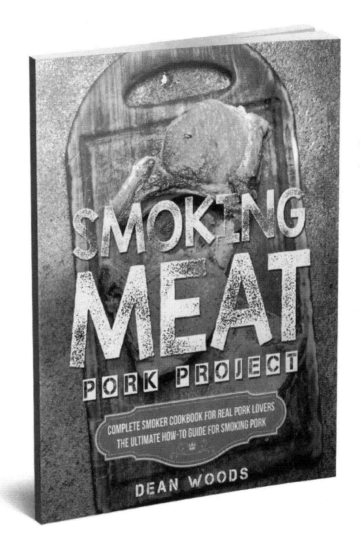

https://www.amazon.com/dp/B078C6HNJF

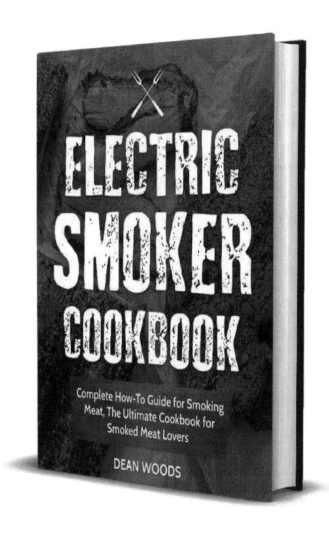

https://www.amazon.com/dp/1725606178

P.S. Thank you for reading this book. If you've enjoyed this book, please don't shy, drop me a line, leave a feedback or both on Amazon. I love reading reviews and your opinion is extremely important for me.

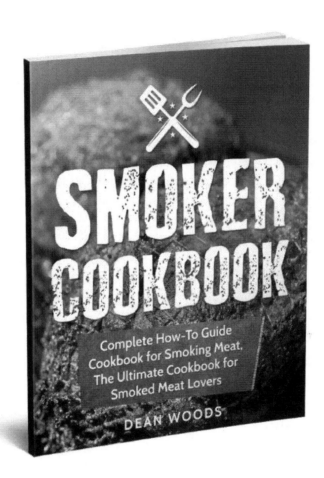

Made in the USA
Middletown, DE
20 December 2019

81534821R00073